KNOTS

KNOTS

STRATHEARN BOOKS LIMITED
Toronto, Canada

Published by Strathearn Books Limited
36 Northline Road
Toronto, Ontario
Canada, M4B 3E2

Copyright ©1998 Quantum Books Ltd
This edition printed 1999

ISBN 1-86160-313-4

This book is produced by
Quantum Books Ltd
6 Blundell Street
London N7 9BH

Project Manager: Rebecca Kingsley
Project Editor: Judith Millidge
Design/Editorial: David Manson
Andy McColm, Maggie Manson

The material in this publication previously appeared in
Knots

QUMSPKN
Set in Futura
Reproduced in Singapore by Eray Scan Pte Ltd
Printed in Singapore by Star Standard Industries (Pte) Ltd

Contents

TYING KNOTS

A knot is simply a connection in a thread, cord or rope which is formed either by passing one free end through a loop and drawing it tight or by tying together or intertwining pieces of threads, cord or rope. There are several quite distinct groups of knot, but they all have one thing in common – the more tightly you can tie them, the greater the strain they are able to withstand before slipping.

Rope Manufacture

Until about the time of World War 2, rope was made from natural materials – hemp and manilla, cotton, coir, flax and sisal. Now, a range of synthetic fibers means that there is a specialized rope for every application.

ROPEMAKING

Traditionally made rope is formed of the fibers of materials that have been twisted together. If you look at an ordinary piece of three-strand rope, you will find that it is laid right-handed. In other words, no matter which way up you hold it, the strands appear to ascend upward and to the right. This is because when it is made, the first group of fibers that are twisted will form right-handed yarn. The yarn is then twisted together in the opposite direction in order to form left-hand strands. The strands are finally then twisted together to form right-laid rope.

The tension that is created by the alternate direction of the twists is recognized as what holds the rope together and provides its in-built strength. It can be seen that even when a strand is uncoiled from the rope, the remaining two strands will cling together, leaving a clearly defined gap in which the missing strand should lie. The way a separated strand is laid-up is a vital concept to grasp, for it is the fundamental principle on which ropemaking is based.

Below. Whichever way you examine right hand laid rope, notice how the strands always ascend upward and to the right. Left hand laid rope is a rarity.

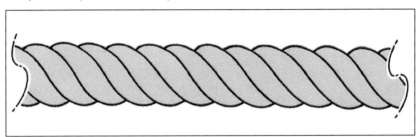

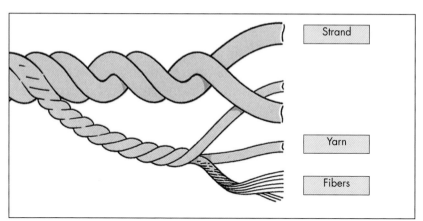

Above. Rope is made up of fibers twisted together, each in the opposite direction to the previous one to form yarn; these are twisted together the opposite way to form strands which in turn are twisted to form right-laid rope.

NATURAL FIBER ROPES

Most rope made from natural fibers is three-strand and right-laid. Left-hand rope is much scarcer and is often four-strand. There is also a six-strand rope, which is made in France, but this type of rope has a hollow core, which has to be filled with cheap stuff. Four-strand rope is approximately 10 percent weaker than its three-strand equivalent, and remarkably, cable-laid line (that is three three-strand ropes laid up left-handed to form a nine-strand cable is 40 percent weaker than the same size of hawser laid (that is, ordinary three-strand) rope.

However, there are seen to be many obvious problems which are associated with natural fiber rope. When wet, it swells, making it extremely difficult to untie the knot – and the rope also tends to become quite brittle. Elements such as harsh sun and chemicals also tend to weather the rope.

Even though natural rope is strong, it is not as strong as it would be if the fibers ran the whole length of the rope. Synthetic ropes on the other hand, can be made from one continuous length. The filaments do not have to be twisted together to make them more coherent.

Types of Rope

A wide range of synthetic ropes has been developed since World War 2, but all share some characteristics: size for size, they are lighter than ropes made from natural fibers, they are available in a variety of colors and they are cheaper than natural rope fibers.

SYNTHETIC STRENGTHS

In addition, synthetic ropes have a high tensile strength and very good load-bearing qualities; they are capable of absorbing shocks; they are immune to rot, mildew and degradation from salt water; they are resistant to chemical damage and corrosion from oils, petrol and most solvents. Moreover, because they absorb less water than ropes made from natural fibers, their breaking strains remain more constant when they are wet.

Commonly Used Rope

Polypropylene

Natural cord

Kernmantel (2-braided)

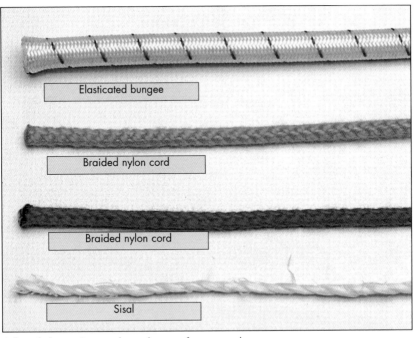

| Elasticated bungee |
| Braided nylon cord |
| Braided nylon cord |
| Sisal |

Left and above. Commonly used types of rope are shown.

SYNTHETIC ROPE TYPES

Nylon (polyamide) ropes are strong and stretch, which make them useful for towing. Nylon ropes also absorb shock loads extremely well, and they do not float. Polyester ropes, on the other hand, provide very little stretch, although they are nearly as strong as nylon ropes. Polypropylene is used to make a popular general purpose rope, which is often used by sailors, but it floats which may rule it out for some instances.

Polyethylene rope is not as strong as other types of synthetic rope and is not widely used. One of the strongest of the many synthetic substances is aramide, but it is expensive and sensitive to ultraviolet light.

The main disadvantage of synthetic ropes, however, is that they are so smooth that some knots slip undone. So knots tied with synthetic rope may need to be secured with an extra half hitch or tuck.

Choosing a Rope

Rope should be chosen according to the situation for which it will be used – considering very carefully both the material with which the rope is made and the type of rope. Some ropes are unsuitable for certain types of activity. The table below provides a summary.

SEALING ENDS

If you buy a length of synthetic rope from a chandlery, to cut the length that you require, they will have to use an electrically heated knife which will shorten the rope to the required length. This will provide you with a sharp edge and will also seal the end. When you cut synthetic rope yourself, however, you will probably use an ordinary knife and then melt the end with a cigarette lighter or an electric ring.

LOOKING AFTER ROPE

It is sometimes hard to remember, but rope is expensive, so always look after it. When you are using it, try to avoid dragging it over any sharp edges or catching it on rough corners which may damage the rope and break the fibers. Also avoid dragging rope over surfaces where particles of dirt and grit will penetrate the fibers. Do not force rope into harsh kinks as this will also cause distortion. Use floating lines only for rescue work.

Below. Types of rope and the purposes to which each type is suited.

Purpose / Material	General purpose	Climbing	Towing	Anchorage	Mooring	Halyards	Fishing
Polyester				X	X	X	
Nylon	X	X	X	X	X		X
Polypropylene			X		X		

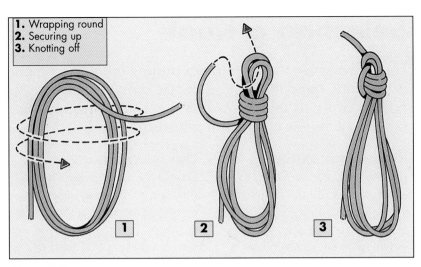

1. Wrapping round
2. Securing up
3. Knotting off

Above. Coiling a rope.

COILING A ROPE

The function of coiling a rope is that the rope will be immediately accessible and untangled when needed. Coiled rope is useful if you want to sling the rope on your backpack or over your shoulder. Before coiling it, always make sure that the rope is dry, even if it is synthetic. If the rope has been in sea water, make sure you rinse it with fresh water in order to remove any deposits of salt that may have penetrated the fibers. At the end of the season, remember to wash all ropes thoroughly in a detergent, making sure that you carefully remove any oil or tar stains with gasoline or trichloroethylene.

KNOTS WEAKEN ROPE

The very act of tying knots will actually weaken a rope. The sharper the curve and the tighter the nip, the greater is the chance that the rope will break, and when it does, it will break immediately outside the knot. Curiously, it is a little known fact that many often-used knots can be surprisingly harmful to rope. One of the worst offenders is seen to be the simple overhand knot (you are able to read more details of this knot if you refer to page 18). *Remember!* Never use two ropes of different material together because only the more rigid of the two will work under strain.

Selecting a Knot

There are several quite distinct groups of knot – hitches and bends, binding knots, stopper knots, knots that form nooses or loops and knots that join small lines together. Each knot serves a different purpose.

KNOW YOUR KNOTS

Although it is not necessary to know a large number of different knots – four or five should suffice in most circumstances – it is very important to know which knot is best suited to the conditions in which it is to be used. You should also bear in mind that any knot will reduce the breaking strain of a line by between 5 and 20 percent.

CHOOSE THE RIGHT KNOT

One of the main reasons for the selection of one knot rather than another is the relative strength of the knots. This is especially true for climbers and mountaineers, but is also a consideration for mariners. Climbers generally use knots that are bulky with several wrapping turns, designed to absorb strains and to avoid weakening the rope.

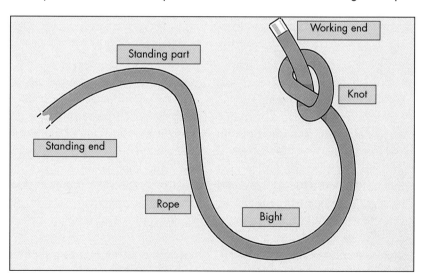

Working end

Standing part

Knot

Standing end

Rope

Bight

Left. The various parts of the rope are shown with their names.

Above. Remember – just before it breaks, a knot slips. The tighter it is tied the better.

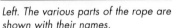

STOPPER KNOTS This group of knots is most often used to prevent the end of a length of rope or string slipping through an eye or a hole. Stopper knots can also be used to bind the end of a line so that it will not unravel. They are frequently used at sea and also used by climbers, campers and fishermen.

HITCHES These knots are used to secure a rope to a post, hook, ring, spar or rail or to another rope that plays no part in the actual tying. Because they are often used by sailors for mooring and fastening, they must be able to withstand parallel strain.

LOOPS Loops are made to be dropped over an object, unlike hitches, which are made directly around the object and follow its shape. Sailors find loops, especially the bowline, indispensable.

BENDS Bends are used to join the ends of two lengths of rope to form one longer piece. To ensure a secure join, ideally the two ropes should be the same kind and diameter.

RUNNING KNOTS These knots are also known as slip knots or nooses. Their main characteristics are that they tighten around objects on which they are tied but slacken when the strain is reduced. Running knots must be among the oldest knots. They were used by man in prehistoric times to make weapons and snares.

SHORTENINGS These invaluable knots are used to shorten long lines. A rope which has been shortened by means of a knot can always be lengthened at a later date. Shortenings can also be used to take up weakened or damaged lengths of line so that they are not subjected to any strain. These useful knots are well worth mastering.

FISHING KNOTS Wet and windy river bank conditions are not ideal for attempting to tie a knot for the first time. It is important therefore that fishermen thoroughly master the art of tying a variety of knots *before* they set out. Any knot must be secure to be useful, which requires endless practice.

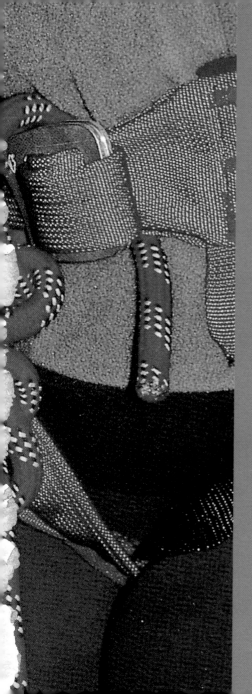

KNOT
TYPES

KEY TO SYMBOLS

Each entry is accompanied by various
icons which provide you with a snapshot
of information about the particular
uses of each knot

 General
purpose

 Camping

 Climbing

 Sailing

 Fishing

OVERHAND KNOT

This is the knot that forms the basis of
most other knots. In its own right it is
used as a simple stopper knot
in the end of a line. It is not,
however, widely used by sailors
as it is difficult to untie when the
rope is wet.

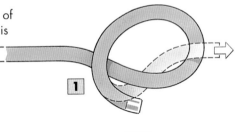

Other names Thumb knot.
Usage
- General purpose.
- Camping.
- Sailing.
- Fishing.

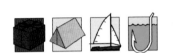

OVERHAND LOOP

This is a rather ungainly knot, but it is
extremely useful in circumstances
where a bulky stopper is
required. It is, in fact, the loop
that most people would tie
without thinking if they
needed to fasten a knot in
the other end of a length of
string. The drawback is that the
line is difficult to untie.

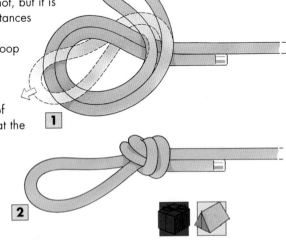

Other names None.
Usage
- General purpose.
- Camping.

MULTIPLE OVERHAND KNOT

This knot's alternative name comes from its use as the knot used to tie in the end of the lashes of a cat o'nine tails, the whip used for flogging in both the British Army and Navy until the punishment's official abolition in 1948. Capuchin monks use this knot to tie their habits. Sailors use the knot as a stopper or weighting knot on small stuff, although it is difficult to untie when wet.

When you tie the knot, keep the loop open and slack, and then pull gently on both ends of the line simultaneously, twisting the two ends in opposite directions as you do so.

Other names Blood knot.
Usage
- General purpose.
- Climbing.
- Camping.
- Sailing.

HEAVING LINE KNOT

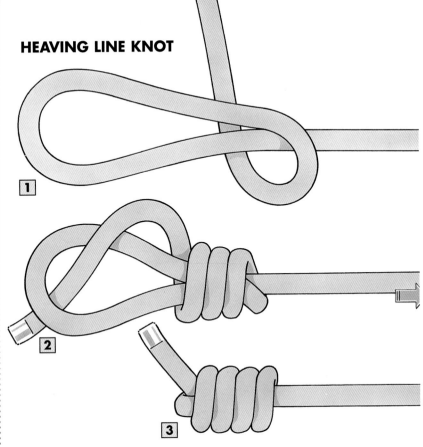

This knot is principally used for sailing when a heavy line is to be thrown ashore or aboard another boat. It is attached to a heaving line – that is, a light line – which can be thrown ahead so that the heavier line can be pulled across the gap. The knot is tied to the end of the lighter line to add additional weight. Heaving lines are up to $3/4$in in diameter and up to 80ft long. They should float and be flexible, and able to bear a man's weight.

Other names Franciscan knot, monk's knot.

Usage
- General purpose.
- Camping.
- Sailing.

FIGURE EIGHT KNOT

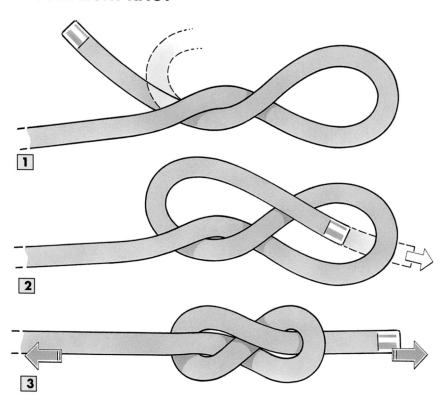

1

2

3

This interlacing knot has for long been regarded as an emblem of interwoven affection, appearing in heraldry as the symbol of faithful love. It also appears in the arms of the House of Savoy.

The knot, which is made in the end of a line, with the upper loop around the standing part and the lower loop around the working end, is widely used by sailors on the running rigging.

Other names Flemish knot, Savoy knot.

Usage
- General purpose.
- Climbing.
- Camping.
- Sailing.

21

HIGHWAYMAN'S HITCH

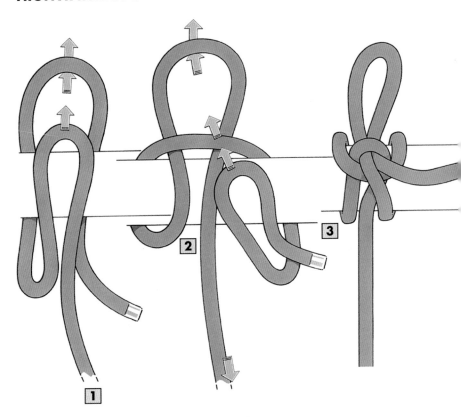

1

2

3

The name highwayman's hitch comes from the fact the knot was supposedly used by robbers to insure a swift release for their horse's reins and thus a rapid get-away. A single pull on the working end unties the knot, but the standing part can safely be put under tension.

Other names Draw hitch.
Usage
- General purpose.
- Camping.

H I T C H E S

22

HALF HITCH

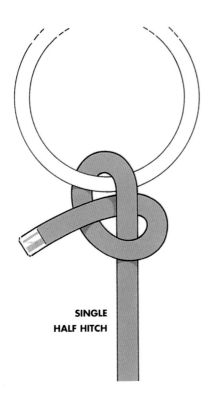

SINGLE HALF HITCH

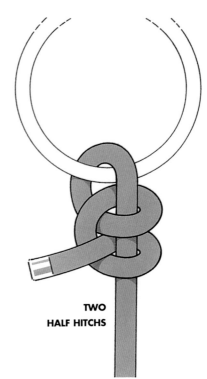

TWO HALF HITCHS

The half hitch is among the most widely used of fastenings, but it is, in fact, a temporary knot, formed of a single hitch made around the standing part of another hitch – as in a round turn and two half hitches, for example. The knot is not meant to take any strain but is rather used to complete and strengthen other knots, which may then be used for tying, hanging or hooking.

Other names None.
Usage
- General purpose.
- Climbing.
- Camping.
- Sailing.

23

COW HITCH

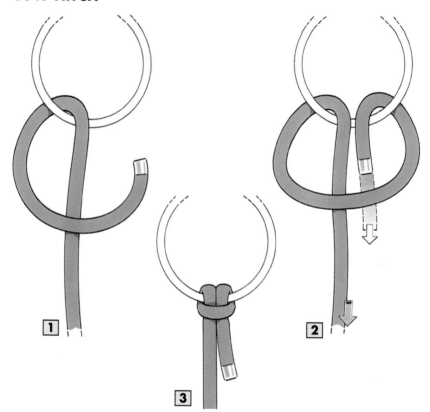

This hitch, composed of two single hitches, is generally made around a ring and is probably the least secure of all the hitches, and it should be regarded as only a temporary fastening. Its name suggests its most common use – as a means of tethering livestock.

Other names Lanyard hitch.
Usage
- General purpose.
- Camping.

TIMBER HITCH

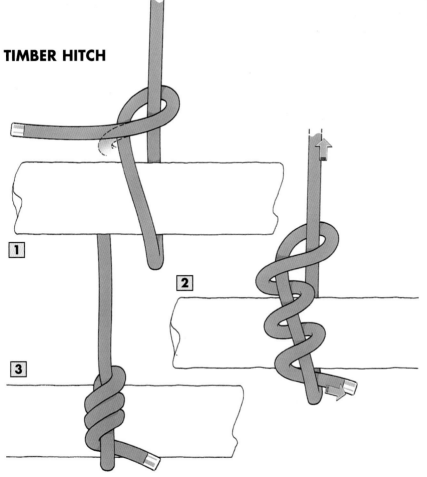

1

2

3

This distinctive-looking knot is really only a temporary noose, formed by twisting the working end around its own part and *not* around the standing part. Three twists are usually sufficient to secure the rope around such objects as tree trunks, planks or poles so that they may be raised or lowered or dragged or pulled. More twists may be needed if the object to be moved is especially thick.

Other names None.
Usage
• General purpose.
• Camping.

TRANSOM KNOT

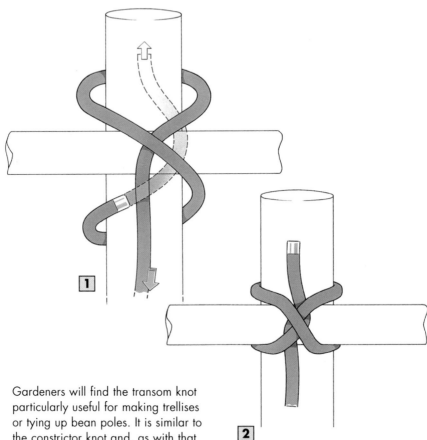

1

2

Gardeners will find the transom knot particularly useful for making trellises or tying up bean poles. It is similar to the constrictor knot and, as with that knot, the ends may be trimmed off for neatness. Although it can be prised undone, it is probably easier simply to cut through the diagonal, when the two halves will fall apart.

Other names None.
Usage
• General purpose.
• Camping.

CONSTRICTOR KNOT

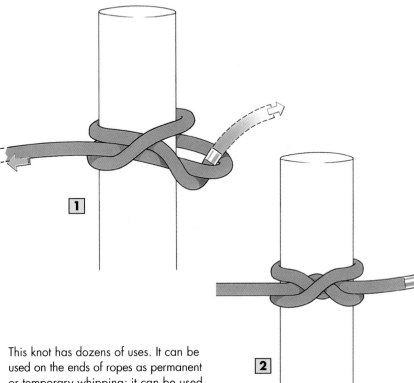

This knot has dozens of uses. It can be used on the ends of ropes as permanent or temporary whipping; it can be used to secure fabric bags; it can be used in woodworking to hold two pieces in position while the glue dries.

The knot is formed from an overhand knot, trapped beneath a crosswise round turn, which holds it firmly in place. The constrictor knot will stay tied and grip firmly in place. The rope may have to be cut free unless the last tuck is made with a bight to produce a slipped knot.

Other names None.
Usage
• General purpose.
• Camping.

CLOVE HITCH

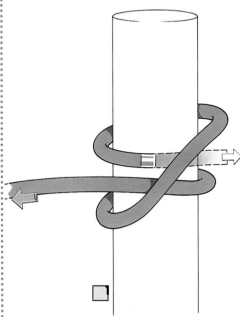

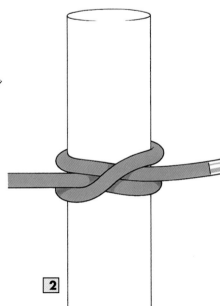

2

The name clove hitch first appeared in Falconer's *Dictionary of the Marine* in the 18th century, but the knot was probably known for centuries before then.

Given practice, the clove hitch can be tied around a post with one hand. It is not totally secure if the strain is intermittent and at an inconsistent angle. Adding a stopper knot or making one or two half hitches around the standing part will make the knot more secure.

Campers often use this knot to secure tent poles, hence the alternative name peg knot.

Other names Boatman's knot, Peg knot.
Usage
• General purpose.
• Climbing.
• Camping.

CLOVE HITCH, DROPPED OVER A POST

The knot formed when two overlapping half hitches are dropped over a post is widely used in sailing for mooring to bollards on docksides. It is also useful in camping for tightening guy ropes.

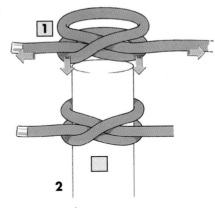

Other names None.
Usage
• Camping.
• Sailing.

CLOVE HITCH, MADE ON A RING

This version of the clove hitch is more commonly used in mountaineering than in sailing, for in sailing the ring is usually narrower than the rope, which can become badly chafed and therefore dangerous. Climbers use it to regulate the length of rope between the climber and the piton (the peg or spike driven into a rock or a crack to hold the rope).

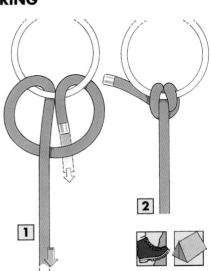

Other names None.
Usage
• Climbing.
• Camping.

FISHERMAN'S BEND

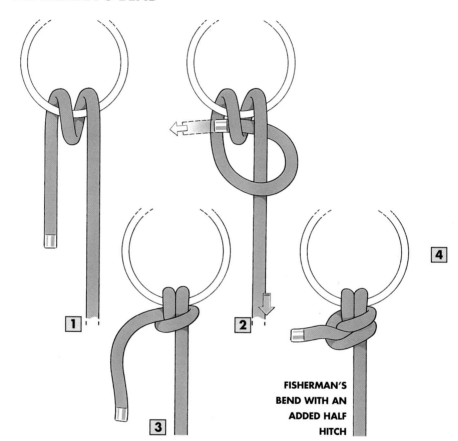

1

2

3

4

**FISHERMAN'S
BEND WITH AN
ADDED HALF
HITCH**

If the cow hitch is the least secure of the hitches, the fisherman's bend is the most stable. Simply formed by making two turns around the post or through the ring and then tucking the working end through both turns, the knot is widely used by sailors to moor their boats at the quayside. Extra security can be achieved by adding a half hitch.

Other names Anchor bend.
Usage
• General purpose.
• Sailing.

CAT'S PAW

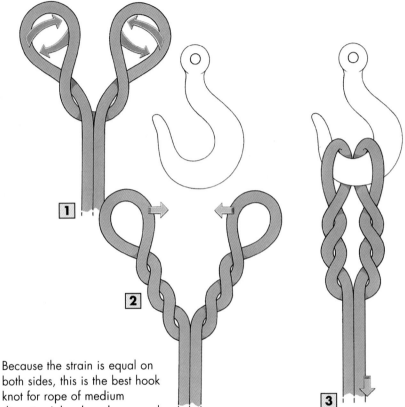

Because the strain is equal on both sides, this is the best hook knot for rope of medium diameter. It has long been used by dock workers and sailors to sling heavy loads, and the name cat's paw has been used since the 18th century. When a single part of a loaded rope is hung over a hook, the line is weakened by about one-third. This knot gives the extra assurance that should one leg break, the other will last long enough to allow the load to be safely lowered to the ground.

Other names None.
Usage
• General purpose.
• Sailing.

BILL HITCH

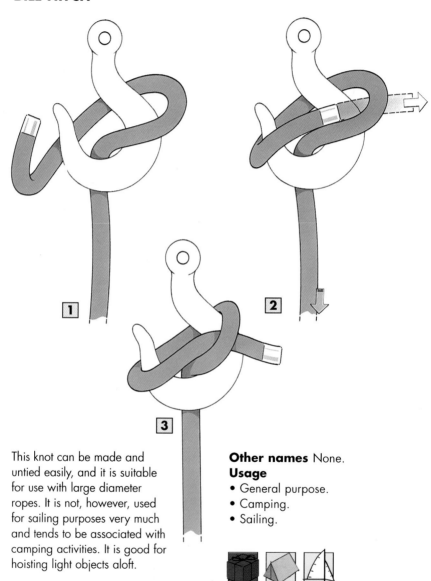

1

2

3

This knot can be made and untied easily, and it is suitable for use with large diameter ropes. It is not, however, used for sailing purposes very much and tends to be associated with camping activities. It is good for hoisting light objects aloft.

Other names None.
Usage
- General purpose.
- Camping.
- Sailing.

ROLLING HITCH

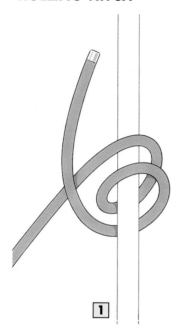

1

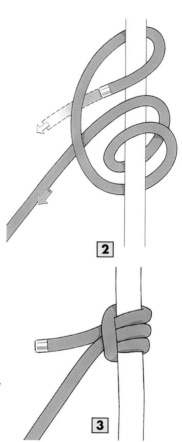

2

3

This is basically a clove hitch with the first turn repeated. It is employed by both mariners and mountaineers and is the most effective way of securing a small rope to a larger line that is under strain. As long as the smaller rope is perpendicular to the larger, the knot will slide easily along; once tension is exerted on the standing part and working end of the smaller rope, the knot locks into position. If you place your hand over the knot and slide it along the thicker line it will slide off the end and uncoil into a straight length of rope.

Other names Magner's hitch, Magnus hitch.

Usage
• Climbing.
• Sailing.

ROUND TURN & TWO HALF HITCHES

Use this versatile knot to fasten a line to a ring, hook, handle, pole, rail or beam. It is a strong, dependable knot, which never jams. It has the additional advantage that once one end has been secured with a round turn and two half hitches, the other end can be tied with a second knot.

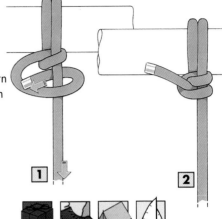

Other names None.
Usage
• General purpose.
• Climbing.
• Camping.
• Sailing.

ITALIAN HITCH

This knot was introduced in 1974, and is the official means of belaying (fixing a running rope around a rock or cleat) of the *Union Internationale des Associations d'Alpinisme*. The rope is passed around and through a carabiner and will check a climber's fall by locking up. The rope can also be pulled in to provide slack or tension as needed. Care must be taken to tie this knot correctly.

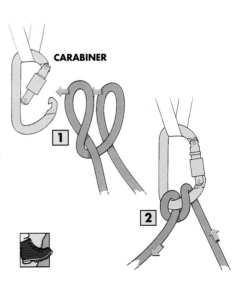

CARABINER

Other names Munter friction hitch, sliding ring hitch.
Usage
• Climbing.

H I T C H E S

PRUSIK KNOT

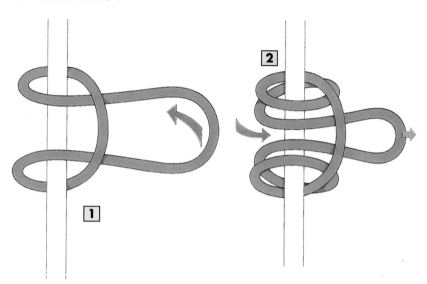

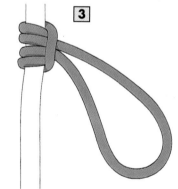

This knot is named after Dr Carl Prusik, who devised it in 1931. Relatively simple to tie, this knot is used by climbers to attach slings to rope so that they slide smoothly when the knot is loose but hold firm when a sideways load is imposed. This is a useful knot for anyone who must scale awkward heights, such as tree surgeons, and cavers.

The knot must be tied to a rope that is considerably thinner than the line around which it is tied, and it is important to note that it may slip if the rope is wet or icy.

Other names None.
Usage
• Climbing.

FIGURE EIGHT LOOP

Although this knot is difficult to adjust and cannot be easily untied after loading, its advantages outweigh these drawbacks. It is a relatively simple knot to tie, and it stays tied. In addition, as its appearance is unmistakable, it can be quickly checked, an important feature for climbers.

Other names Figure eight on the bight
Usage
- General purpose.
- Climbing.
- Camping.
- Sailing.

THREADED FIGURE EIGHT

This is a variation of the figure eight loop. The most frequent uses of the threaded figure eight are for tying on to the rope and for anchoring non-climbing members of a team.

This is probably the commonest way of attaching rope to the harness. Tying-on using a Bowline is equally satisfactory, but not as popular.

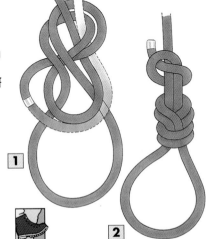

Other names None.
Usage
- Climbing.

LOOPS

BOWLINE

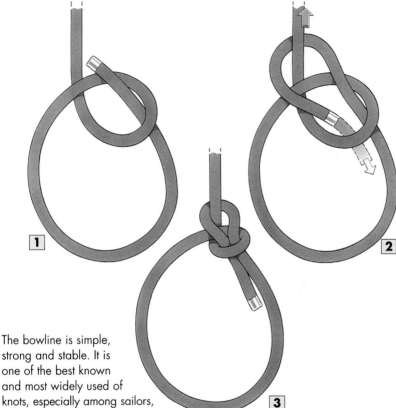

1

2

3

The bowline is simple, strong and stable. It is one of the best known and most widely used of knots, especially among sailors, and is generally tied to form a fixed loop at the end of a line or to attach a rope to an object.

For safety's sake, finish the bowline off with a stopper knot to prevent it from turning into a slip knot. If tied with stiff rope, it is liable to work loose as the line cannot 'bed down' properly.

The running bowline makes a noose that falls open as soon as the tension is removed from the line.

Other names None.
Usage
• Climbing.
• Camping.
• Sailing.

L
O
O
P
S

37

BOWLINE, CASTING METHOD

Use the method of tying a bowline illustrated here when you need to fasten a line around an object. When synthetic rope is used to tie this knot, it might be less reliable. It is a good idea to secure the end with an extra half-hitch, or tuck it and trap it beneath one of the rope's strands.

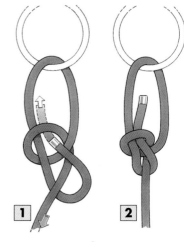

Other names None.
Usage
• Climbing.
• Camping.
• Sailing.

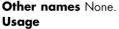

CLIMBER'S BOWLINE

Climbers use this bowline as a safety measure during ascents, when it is clipped into the carabiner.

Climbers also tie this knot directly around their waists so that they can adjust the length of line before undertaking an ascent. Whenever it is used in this way, the knot must be finished off with a stopper knot.

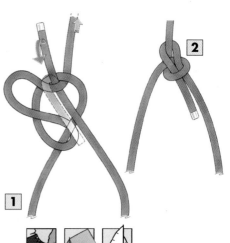

Other names Bulin knot.
Usage
• Climbing.
• Camping.
• Sailing.

L O O P S

BOWLINE ON A BIGHT

This is an ancient knot, still in use today, especially in sea rescues. If the person who is being rescued is conscious, he or she places a leg through each loop and hangs on to the standing part.

If the casualty is unconscious, both legs are placed through one loop while the other loop is passed under the armpits.

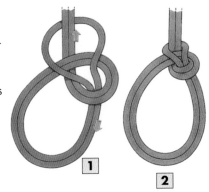

Other names None.
Usage
- General purposes.
- Climbing.
- Camping.
- Sailing.

BOWLINE, ROPE UNDER TENSION

This knot is often used by sailors to attach boats to rings. The standing part remains taut throughout, while the working end is tied to create a secure fastening.

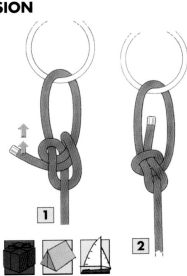

Other names None.
Usage
- General purposes.
- Camping.
- Sailing.

SPANISH BOWLINE

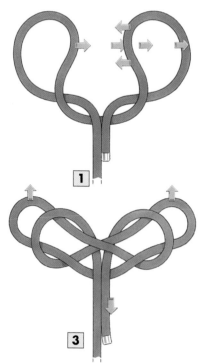

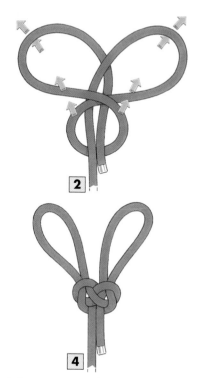

This is an extremely strong knot that is used by firemen, coastguards and mountain rescuers. Like the bowline on a bight, it is an ancient knot, which is formed of two separate and independent loops that hold securely, even under considerable strain. One loop is slipped over the casualty's head, around the back and under the armpits; the other loop goes around both legs, just behind the knees. Each loop must be adjusted to size and locked in position or the casualty could easily fall through the loops.

Other names Chair knot.
Usage
- General purpose.
- Climbing.
- Camping.
- Sailing.

ANGLER'S LOOP

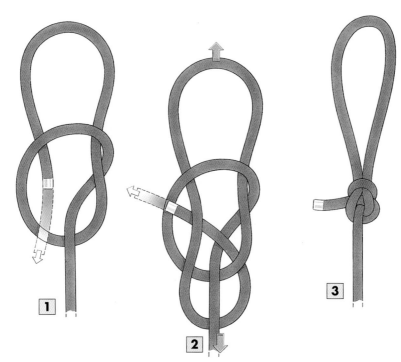

1

2

3

This knot is known to have been in use since the 1870s. It is, as its name suggests, most used by fishermen. In addition to fishing line, it can be tied with string or fine synthetic line. Authorities differ about whether it is a suitable knot for rope. It is difficult to untie, which may militate against its use at sea, and it is prone to jam. It is also a rather bulky knot.

Other names Perfection loop.
Usage
• Camping.
• Fishing.

THREE-PART CROWN

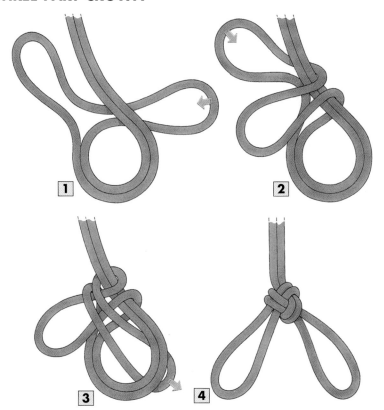

This is a secure knot, but it is not generally used by sailors because it is difficult to untie after it has supported a heavy weight. It is sometimes used by campers to hang food and equipment. It can also be used as a decorative knot from which to hang objects.

Other names None.
Usage
• General purposes.
• Camping.

ALPINE BUTTERFLY KNOT

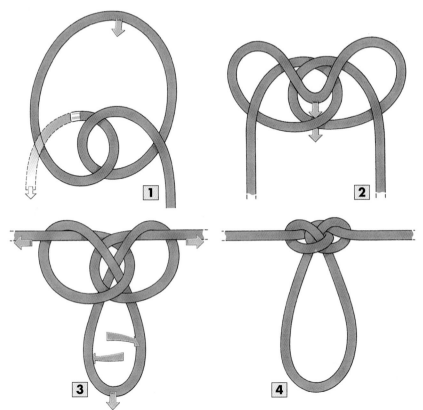

This symmetrical knot is sometimes used by climbers, who loop it around the chest. It will hold equally well whichever end is held; it can be tied quickly; the loop does not shrink when the knot is tightened; and it can be easily untied. Its main disadvantage is that it is difficult to tie and with the increased use of the Italian hitch, the Alpine Butterfly knot has lost much of its popularity.

Other names None.
Usage
• Climbing.

REEF KNOT

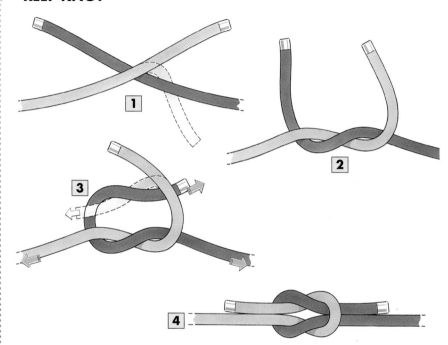

This is an knot that the Ancient Greeks knew as the Hercules knot. It is often the only knot that people know – apart from the granny knot. When the ends are only partly drawn through the knot to leave loops and to form a double reef bow, it is frequently use to tie shoe laces. The traditional use is for joining the two ends of a rope when reefing a sail.

This knot should only be used as a temporary measure and with lines of the same diameter that will not be subject to strain. If the lines must bear any weight, then stopper knots must be tied in the short ends.

Other names Square knot.
Usage
• General purpose.
• Camping.
• Sailing.

CAPSIZED REEF KNOT

The ease with which a reef knot can be slipped apart made it perfect for reefing sails. When one end of a reef knot is pulled sharply or subjected to strain, the knot will untie and become unstable. Capsized reef knots have caused accidents and should be used with caution.

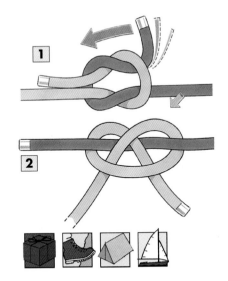

Other names Lark's head knot, capsized square knot.
Usage
• General purpose.
• Camping.
• Sailing.

THIEF KNOT

According to legend, sailors on whaling ships used this knot to tie their clothes bags. Thieves would retie them with reef knots, thus revealing that the bags had been burgled. The thief knot is very similar to the reef knot, but the short ends are on opposite sides.

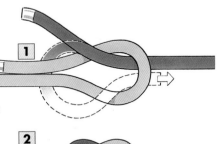

Other names None.
Usage
• General purpose.

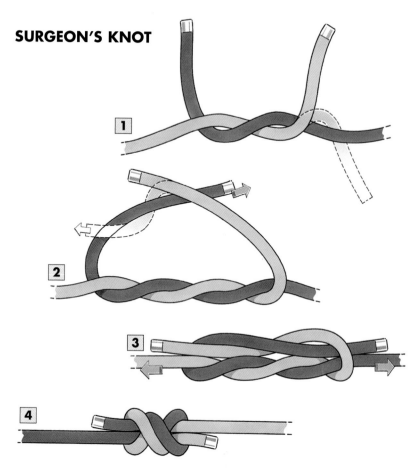

SURGEON'S KNOT

1

2

3

4

As it names suggests, this knot is used by surgeons to tie off blood vessels, and it seems to have been in use since about the end of World War 2. The knot has a good grip, twisting as it is drawn up and the diagonal is wrapped around it. It is less bulky and flatter than some of the other knots used by surgeons – the carrick bend and the reef knot, for instance – which tend to leave visible scars.

Other names None.
Usage
• General purpose.
• Fishing.

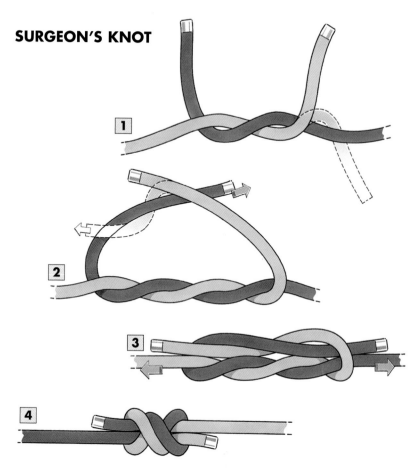

BENDS

46

FISHERMAN'S KNOT

Not to be confused with the fisherman's bend, this knot is formed from two identical overhand knots. These are pushed against each other so that the short, working ends of rope lie in opposite directions. Used to join lines of equal diameter.

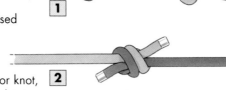

Other names Angler's knot, English knot, Englishman's bend or knot, Halibut knot, True-lover's bend or knot, Waterman's knot.

Usage
• Climbing.
• Camping.
• Fishing.

DOUBLE FISHERMAN'S KNOT

This is one of the strongest knots for joining ropes or for forming slings, and it is used not only, as it names suggests, by anglers to secure their lines but also by climbers on small stuff. It is relatively bulky and is not suitable for anything more substantial than thin line or string. The ends can be taped or seized to the working parts to minimize the risk of the knot working loose.

Other names Grapevine knot.
Usage
• Climbing.
• Camping.
• Fishing.

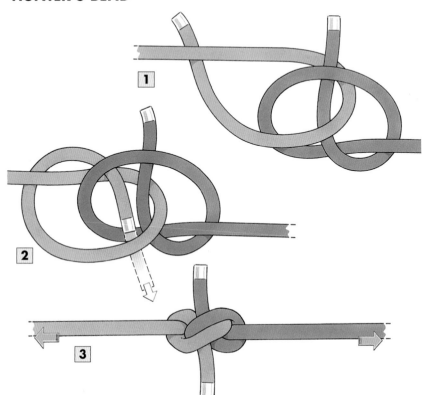

HUNTER'S BEND

Although attributed to Dr E Hunter in 1968, this knot had already been described by a Phil Smith, an American in 1950. Phil Smith had devised the knot during World War 2 and named it Rigger's bend.

It is also easy to untie, based on two overhand knots and is stronger than the fisherman's bend, although it is not as strong as the blood knot.

Other names Rigger's bend.
Usage
• General purpose.
• Camping.

SHEET BEND

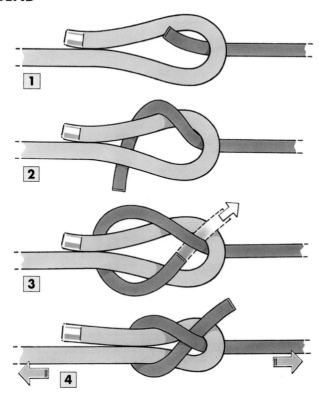

Unusually, this knot can be used to join lines of unequal diameters. Probably the most commonly used bend, it is not 100 percent secure and should not be used where it will be subject to great strain. It can also be used to make a rope fast to anything with an aperture – a handle on a spade, for example.

When the knot is tied with the short ends on opposite sides it becomes a left-handed sheet bend, but this is to be avoided as this knot is not secure.

Other names Common bend, Flag bend.
Usage
• General purpose.
• Camping.
• Sailing.

FIGURE EIGHT BEND

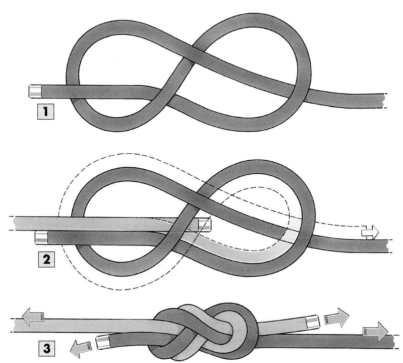

Although this is a simple knot to tie – simply make a figure eight in one end and follow it around with the other working end – it is one of the strongest bends that can be tied in both rope and string.

Other names Flemish bend or knot.

Usage
• General purpose.
• Camping.

B E N D S

CARRICK BEND

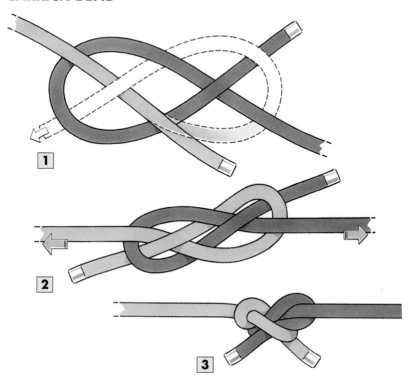

1

2

3

This stable knot is formed from two over-hand loops crossing each other. It was widely used on old sailing ships. It is not commonly used today by sailors as it is difficult to untie when the rope is wet.

In its flat form it is sometimes used to fasten scarves and belts, its symmetrical appearance has made it popular with illustrators of military uniforms.

When drawn up, it capsizes into a completely different shape, making it unsuitable for mountaineer's use as it is too bulky to pass through a carabiner.

Other names Cowboy knot, Split knot, Warp knot.

Usage
- General purpose.
- Climbing.
- Camping.
- Sailing.

RUNNING BOWLINE

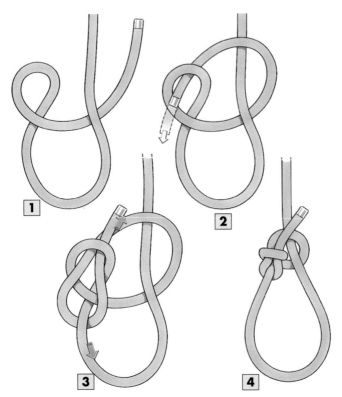

This is probably the running knot to be used by mariners. It is found on the running rigging or it may be used to raise floating objects that have fallen overboard.

It has many uses, being strong and secure, easy to slide and simple to undo. Tying it does not weaken the rope. The knot is mostly used for hanging objects with ropes of unequal diameters. The weight of the object creates the tension needed to make the knot grip.

Other names None.
Usage
• General purpose.
• Climbing.
• Camping.
• Sailing.

HANGMAN'S KNOT

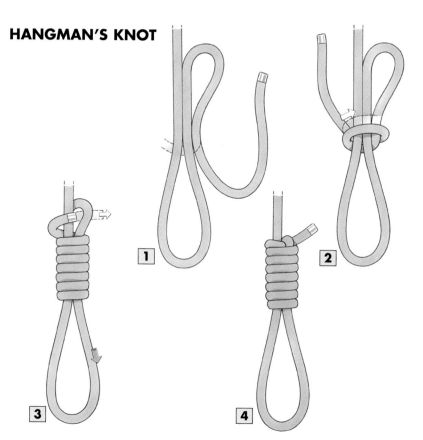

1

2

3

4

This is one of the running knots that is formed by knotting a closed bight at the end of a line. Its name reveals its macabre use, and its alternative name comes from the notorious hangman and executioner Jack Ketch, who died in 1686. It is a strong noose, which slides easily. The number of turns can vary between seven and thirteen, although an odd number should always be used.

Other names Jack Ketch's knot.
Usage
• General purpose.

NOOSE

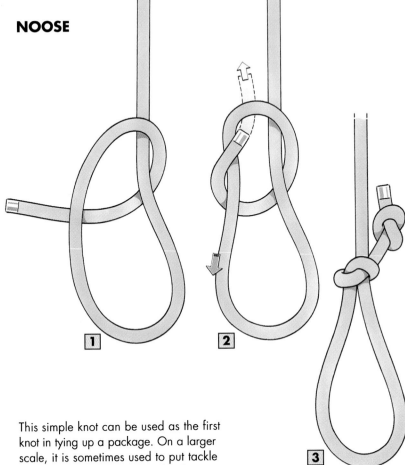

1

2

3

This simple knot can be used as the first knot in tying up a package. On a larger scale, it is sometimes used to put tackle cables under stress. It is made of string or small stuff. The noose can be also used as a hitch as they are very secure.

A noose can also be used when it is difficult to get close to the object around which the knot is to be tied.

A stopper knot should also be added to prevent the noose slipping.

Other names None.
Usage
• General purpose.
• Camping.

TARBUCK KNOT

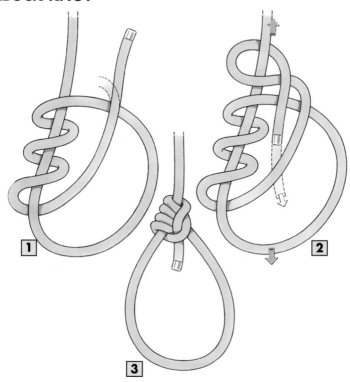

Like the hangman's knot, this knot is formed by knotting a closed bight at the end of a line. It was devised for use by climbers when the rope was likely to be subjected to heavy or unexpected stress because the knot absorbed the shock. The introduction of double-braid ropes which can absorb any shocks, has lessened the use of this knot.

This is still a useful general purpose knot, which grips under strain although it can slide along the standing part. It is not, however, a very secure knot.

Other names None.
Usage
• General purpose.
• Camping.

SHEEP SHANK

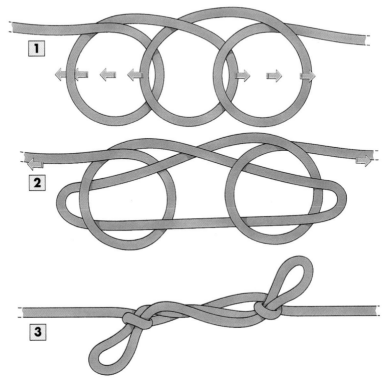

This is a seafarer's knot, easily tied and holds under tension. The number of half hitches can vary from three to five, and that number determines both the firmness of the grip of the knot and the length by which the line is shortened.

This knot is also used at sea for towing boats and on the running rigging. It can also be used to keep slack lines out of the way. When the knot is used to shorten a damaged line, it is important that the damaged section of rope passes through both of the half hitches.

Other names None.
Usage
• Camping.
• Sailing.

SHORTENINGS

LOOP KNOT

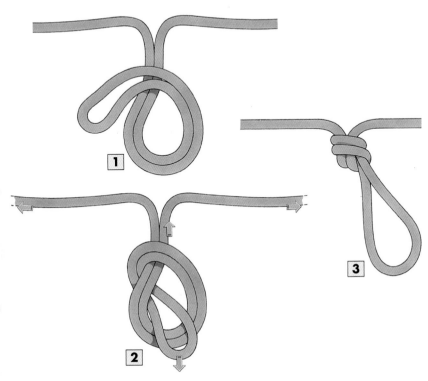

One of the best ways of shortening a damaged rope is to tie a loop knot. This simple fastening takes up the weakened part of the line in the center of the knot so that it is not put under strain. The knot is often used for towing cars and trucks.

Other names None.
Usage
• General purpose.
• Camping.

BLOOD KNOT

This knot has a relatively high breaking strain and is widely used to tie nylon line in a host of situations.

When you tie a blood knot, it is best to leave it slack so that you can count the turns. This will mean that the ends will have to be cut neatly, but the grip is excellent.

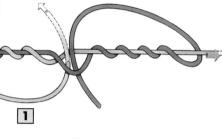

1

2

Other names Barrel knot.
Usage
• Fishing.

BLOOD LOOP DROPPER KNOT

When fishermen want more than one fly on a line at the same time, they use a weighted line with a series of hooks at intervals along it. Additional flies are known as droppers, and this is the loop that is used to attach them to a paternoster because the loop is formed at a right angle to the line.

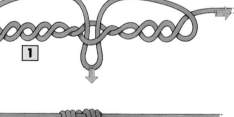

1

2

Other names Dropper loop.
Usage
• Fishing.

HALF-TUCKED BLOOD KNOT

Anglers use this knot when they need to tie a swivel or eyed hook to their lines. It is an easy knot to master and can be tied quickly. However, it is only really successful when it is used with fine monofilament. This is not a suitable knot for heavy lines.

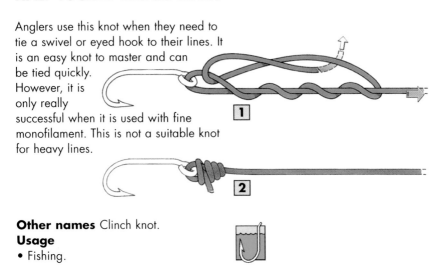

Other names Clinch knot.
Usage
• Fishing.

TURLE KNOT

This knot is used by fishermen to tie flies with turned-up or turned-down eyes to the tippet. It is not suitable for use with ring-eye hooks. The knot was named after Major Turle of Devon, England, in 1884. The line is passed through the eye of the hook, the knot is tied and then the hook is drawn through the loop of the knot.

Other names None.
Usage
• Fishing.

WATER KNOT

The earliest printed reference to this knot
is believed to be in 1496. It is useful
because it can be used to join lines
of different sizes. The breaking
strength can be even further
enhanced by tucking the ends
three or more times to create a
quadruple overhand knot with both lines
and then drawing then carefully together
as you would a multiple overhand knot.

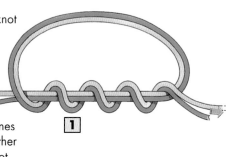

Other names Cove knot.
Usage
• Fishing.

GRINNER KNOT

This is an excellent and justifiably popular
knot for joining either a fly or an eyed
hook to a leader (that is a length of
nylon that forms the junction
between the
fly-line and the
fly) or to a tippet
(the thin, terminal section of a leader).

Other names Duncan loop knot,
Uni-knot.
Usage
• Fishing.

DOUBLE GRINNER KNOT

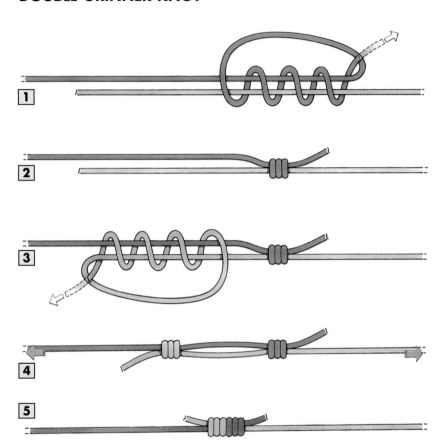

This knot is actually two grinner or uni-knots tied back to back. It is used by fishermen who are trying to catch large fish with small flies on very fine tippets as it is an effective way of joining together two sections of a tippet or a leader.

Other names Paragum knot.
Usage
• Fishing.

DOUBLE LOOP KNOT

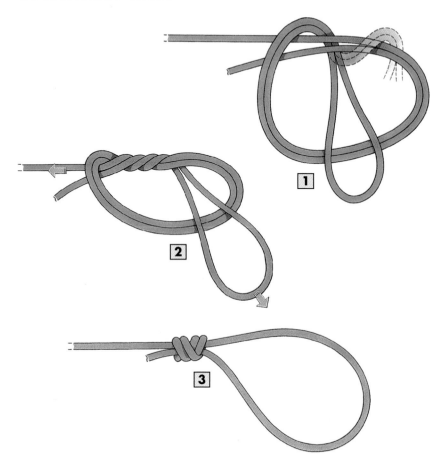

1

2

3

This knot is tied in the same way as the surgeon's knot except that it is made with a single length of line. This non-slip loop can be tied very quickly.

Other names Surgeon's loop.
Usage
• General purpose.
• Fishing.

NEEDLE KNOT

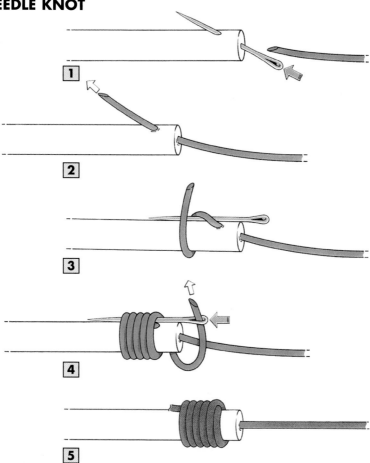

The needle knot is used to effect a smooth join between the fly-line and the butt end (that is, the thick part) of the leader. Not only is this an extremely strong way of fastening monofilament to a fly-line, it is also unlikely to catch or snag on debris as the line is fished.

Other names Needle nail knot.
Usage
• Fishing.

Index

INDEX